Bushfires

Written by Kerrie Shanahan

Flying Start
to Literacy®

Contents

Introduction

A bushfire is a powerful force. It can burn rapidly in the countryside or the wilderness. And it can quickly get out of control.

Flames as tall as a four-storey building reach high into the sky. Strong winds fan the flames and the fire reaches incredible speeds. The fire moves much faster than a person can run. It races through forests and roars up hills, burning everything in its path. It jumps over ditches, roads and rivers.

The heat of the fire can destroy buildings. It can cause glass to explode and metal to melt. Sparks and flying embers shoot far ahead of the fire and start new fires where they fall. Thick smoke fills the sky, blocking the sun and turning day to night.

Fire Fact

Bushfires are also called wildfires in some countries.

Thick smoke fills the air during a bushfire.

Chapter 1:

From spark to inferno

How do fires start?

A single spark can start a fire. Some fires start naturally. The first spark that starts a fire can come from a lightning strike. Or a fire can start when a spark is caused by falling rocks.

Many fires are started by accident. Sparks from machinery or a campfire left smouldering can start a bushfire.

Some fires are lit on purpose. This is called arson and it is against the law.

Fire Fact

Fire burns more quickly as it races up a hill and slows down as it burns down a hill.

The material that burns in a fire is called fuel. Trees, undergrowth, grass and buildings all make good fuel for bushfires, and if there is a lot of fuel, the fire will grow quickly. If there is nothing to burn, it will stop.

A fire also needs oxygen to keep burning. If a fire has no oxygen, it will slow and eventually stop.

There is a lot of fuel for this bushfire.

A raging inferno

Bushfires spread more rapidly when the weather is hot and dry. The hot sun dries up any moisture in the trees and plants, making them crisp, dry and easy to burn.

The bushfire grows and moves rapidly as strong winds fan the flames. The wind blows embers and burning pieces of plants ahead of the fire, which can start new blazes called spot fires.

8

Direction of a bushfire

The fire front burns the fastest and gets the hottest.

The sides of the fire are called the flanks. Flanks move more slowly, but if there is a sudden wind change a flank can become a fire front.

Chapter 2:

Being prepared for fire

In some places, bushfires are an unavoidable part of nature. But there are many ways people can prepare for a bushfire.

National parks and bush areas are high-fire-danger zones because they have a lot of dead wood as well as small trees and bushes that burn easily in a bushfire.

This firefighter is burning dry grass that would catch fire quickly during a bushfire.

Forestry workers burn some areas of bush at times of the year when fires cannot spread too quickly. This helps to reduce the amount of fuel that would burn during a bushfire.

During the winter months when the risk of bushfires is low, firefighters work hard to maintain their equipment, making sure it is ready for an emergency. They continue to train and learn about fires.

Fire Fact

The world's most fire-prone places are south-eastern Australia, California and the south of France. These places all have long, hot, dry summers.

Getting your house ready

People who live in high-fire-danger areas need to prepare for the fire season. They can remove the old and dry plant litter from their yard to reduce the amount of fuel. This reduces the risk of a flying ember starting a fire in their yard.

They also need a safety plan so they know what to do if a bushfire threatens their house. They should have a fire safety kit containing clothing and equipment such as torches, blankets and towels.

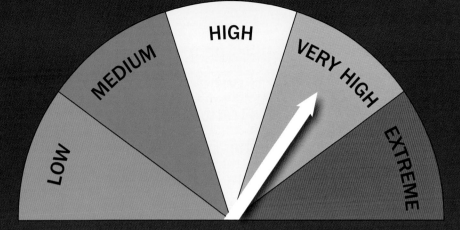

FIRE DANGER TODAY

This sign tells people when there is a high risk of bushfires.

If there is a high risk of fire, the radio and emergency services websites will give people constant fire updates. If people are in an area where a bushfire is approaching, they can be alerted by phone and text message so they know to carry out their safety plan.

Fire Fact

On 9 February 2009, more than 170 people were killed in the Black Saturday bushfires in Victoria.

Early warning

Firefighters try to give people the earliest warning possible. Having an early warning of fire saves lives. Firefighters have a better chance of stopping the fire, and people have the chance to leave their homes and to protect themselves.

Fire spotters are people who are trained to look out for fires. They look out over forests and bush areas from high towers. At the first sign of smoke, they contact the local fire brigade.

Some towers have computerised sensing equipment that can detect smoke and flames. A single sensor can cover 4000 hectares of land. Radar and satellite images are also used to detect early signs of fire.

This fire spotter is looking for smoke in a forest.

This tower is taller than the forest, which makes it easier for fire spotters to see fires.

Chapter 3:

Fighting bushfires

Fighting bushfires is dangerous and can be life threatening. Firefighters have to be strong and brave, as well as highly skilled.

A helicopter dumps water on a bushfire.

Many people work together to bring bushfires under control. Some crews fight the fire on the front line. These crews usually get to the fire front on a fire truck, which is equipped with large water tanks and long hoses.

Some fire crews clear land around the fire to set up a barrier between the fire and unburnt land. This helps to reduce the amount of fuel the fire has to burn, and can help to stop the fire from spreading.

Fires are also attacked from above. Helicopters and air tankers are used to drop large amounts of water on fires. They are also used to drop chemicals that help to stop a fire burning. These chemicals are called fire retardants.

Tracking the fires

Firefighters also use computers and satellites to help fight bushfires. Satellites create images of the fire from above. These images show where the fire hot spots are, where the fire is moving the fastest and where it is slowing down.

This is a satellite image of south-eastern Australia. The black part shows the area that has been burnt by a bushfire.

smoke from a bushfire

Computers use satellite images to calculate the height and temperature of the flames and changes in wind direction. This data is used by fire chiefs to decide where their firefighters should be attacking the fire and how.

Drones

It is dangerous for pilots in aircraft to get too close to a bushfire. Aircraft called drones do not have a pilot on board. They are controlled remotely by firefighters on the ground.

A drone can detect vehicles that might be hidden under trees and the position of dangerous liquids such as petrol. The information collected is sent directly to fire chiefs.

The drone collects information about what is happening under the smoke.

Smoke jumpers

Smoke jumpers are firefighters who are lowered out of a helicopter to fight bushfires in a remote area. Firefighting tools and food and water are dropped near the smoke jumpers. They are equipped to stay and fight the fire for up to 48 hours.

Chapter 4:

Fires in the bush

Bushfires are a part of nature. They play an important role in keeping forests and grassland areas healthy.

How bushfires help

Bushfires help to clear forest floors of dead plants and rotting trees. By burning the forest floor, bushfires make space for new plants to grow.

New plants begin to grow after a bushfire.

Bushfires burn through the thick canopy of leaves that covers a forest, allowing more sunlight to reach the forest floor. This helps more plants to grow.

Bushfires can help seeds to germinate, or begin to grow. Some seeds need the strong heat of a bushfire to break down their thick coating so that they can germinate. Other seeds need a bushfire to clear the forest floor before they can germinate.

Fire Fact

Some plants, such as the banksia tree, have seeds that are encased in thick, woody pods. This helps the seeds to survive a bushfire.

Plants that are native to high-risk bushfire areas are often able to survive bushfires.

Many eucalyptus trees have very thick bark that helps to protect the tree's trunk from fire. Bushfires help to control the growth of plants that are not native to an area, which are often a threat to the native plants.

This eucalyptus tree is growing new leaves after a fire.

This wombat is sheltering in a hollow log that
was burnt out during a bushfire.

The new shoots and plants that grow after
a bushfire provide food for animals in the
forest. And when a bushfire burns the leaves
from trees, it is easier for birds to find the
insects that live in the trees, so the birds
have more food to eat. Bushfires also leave
hollow, burnt-out logs in a forest. These
make good shelters for some animals.

Conclusion

There will always be bushfires, and they can be harmful as well as helpful. People have developed ways to prepare for bushfires and fight them.

Experts are continually learning about the behaviour of bushfires. They are using this knowledge to help people live safely in areas of high fire danger.

Index

A note from the author

I live in a high-fire-danger area. Just over two years ago, a destructive fire raged through small communities not far from where I live. This horrible day reinforced to me the importance of understanding bushfires. I was inspired to write this book so that people can learn more about bushfires and how to be prepared for them.

I found out information by talking to people who have been involved in fighting fires. I also found information on the websites of different firefighting units. Local government websites often have information on how to get ready for the fire season.